Clownfish and Sea Anemones

By Kevin Cunningham

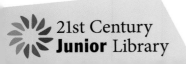
21st Century
Junior Library

Published in the United States of America by
Cherry Lake Publishing
Ann Arbor, Michigan
www.cherrylakepublishing.com

Content Adviser: Stephen Ditchkoff, Professor of Wildlife Ecology and Management, Auburn University, Alabama
Reading Adviser: Marla Conn MS, Ed., Literacy specialist, Read-Ability, Inc.

Photo Credits: © Richard Whitcombe/Shutterstock, cover, 1, 14; © Levent Konuk/Shutterstock, 4; © Kletr/Shutterstock, 6; © Andrey Armyagov/Shutterstock, 8; © Joe Belanger/Shutterstock, 10; © Natural Visions / Alamy Stock Photo, 12; © Vlad61/Shutterstock, 16; © Hans Gert Broeder/Shutterstock, 18; © YUSRAN ABDUL RAHMAN/Shutterstock, 20

Library of Congress Cataloging-in-Publication Data

Names: Cunningham, Kevin, 1966- author.
Title: Clownfish and sea anemones / Kevin Cunningham.
Description: Ann Arbor, MI : Cherry Lake Publishing, [2016] | Series: Better together |
   Audience: K to grade 3. | Includes bibliographical references and index.
Identifiers: LCCN 2015049539| ISBN 9781634710855 (hardcover) | ISBN 9781634712835 (pbk.) |
   ISBN 9781634711845 (pdf) | ISBN 9781634713825 (ebook)
Subjects: LCSH: Mutualism (Biology)—Juvenile literature. | Anemone fishes—Juvenile literature. |
   Sea anemones—Juvenile literature. | Animal behavior—Juvenile literature.
Classification: LCC QH548.3 .C856 2016 | DDC 591.7/85—dc23
LC record available at http://lccn.loc.gov/2015049539

Cherry Lake Publishing would like to acknowledge the work of The Partnership for 21st Century Skills.
Please visit *www.p21.org* for more information.

Printed in the United States of America
Corporate Graphics

CONTENTS

5 **Hide and Sneak**

7 **Meet the Clownfish**

11 **Tentacle Trick**

17 **A Fair Trade**

22 Glossary

23 Find Out More

24 Index

24 About the Author

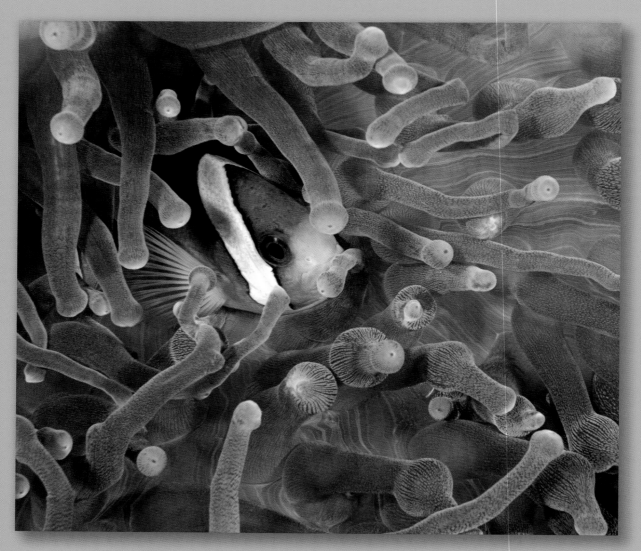

The clownfish and sea anemone are an unlikely pair.

Hide and Sneak

A brightly colored clownfish hides inside the **tentacles** of a sea anemone. The sea anemone uses a **disguise**. Currents in the water make its tentacles sway. It looks like a plant.

Clownfish like to stay at home. A clownfish lives its whole life around the same **coral reef**. The sea anemone does, too.

The clownfish and sea anemone team up. They are **allies**. They help each other survive.

There are 28 species of clownfish. This is the percula clownfish.

Meet the Clownfish

Many kinds of clownfish live in the world's seas. One **species** that teams with sea anemones swims in the western Pacific Ocean. It lives in warm waters. Coral reefs are common in those areas.

The coral reef **ecosystem** creates problems for clownfish. Lots of **predators** live in the coral reefs. The predators want to eat the clownfish. Clownfish cannot swim very fast. They do not have sharp teeth for

Coral reefs can be a dangerous place for a tiny fish.

fighting. Hungry hunters love to feed on clownfish.

The clownfish need help. The sea anemone provides a safe place to stay. Predators fear the sea anemone. They leave the clownfish alone. But why be afraid of something that looks like a plant? It turns out a sea anemone knows how to keep away predators.

Make a Guess!

Humans keep clownfish in fish tanks as pets. Clownfish in tanks live longer than wild clownfish. But they do not grow as big. Why do you think pet clownfish live longer? Why do you think they are smaller?

Sea anemones look like plants, but they eat meat.

Tentacle Trick

The smallest sea anemone species grow to less than 0.5 inches (1 centimeter) long. The largest reach 6 feet (1.8 meters) tall. A sea anemone sticks to a coral reef or a rock with its one leg. It never moves.

Sea anemones are **carnivores**. But a sea anemone doesn't hunt like a shark. It waits for a creature to touch its tentacles. Then it shoots the creature with a tiny dart.

Sea anemones eat small fish and shrimp.

The dart contains **poison**. The poison stuns the creature. It cannot move. The sea anemone uses its tentacles. They move the creature to its mouth. Fish know about sea anemones. They stay away.

But sea anemones leave clownfish alone. Young clownfish know a trick.

Create!

Giacomo Merculiano was an artist. He made brightly colored paintings of sea anemones. Get crayons, colored pencils, or paints. Draw different sizes of sea anemones. Use bright colors. Invent your own species.

A sea anemone doesn't recognize a clownfish as prey when the clownfish is covered in sea anemone mucus.

They rub against the sea anemone's tentacles. **Mucus** on the young clownfish pushes away the poison. At the same time, a clownfish gets sea anemone mucus all over its body. That makes the sea anemone stop attacking. The clownfish can safely hide inside the tentacles.

Butterflyfish are beautiful but they're dangerous to sea anemones.

A Fair Trade

The clownfish does more than hide. It helps out the sea anemone, too.

The butterflyfish eats sea anemones. It is **immune** to sea anemone poison. A clownfish protects its partner. If a butterflyfish swims up, the clownfish chases it away.

Clownfish eat all kinds of food. Their diet includes small ocean animals and plants. Chunks of food float in the water when clownfish eat. The sea anemone draws

Even though they live underwater, clownfish and
sea anemones need oxygen to live.

these scraps to its mouth. Clownfish also eat the sea anemone's scraps. Clownfish and sea anemones even use each other's **waste** to stay healthy.

The two animals take their teamwork further. Sea creatures need **oxygen** just like humans do. Many creatures get it by moving through the water.

Look!

Clownfish live inside sea anemone tentacles to stay safe. Other animals also hide in their homes. Think about where you live. Which animals build homes in the open? Which prefer hidden homes?

Both the sea anemone and the clownfish benefit from this teamwork.

But sea anemones stay in one place. If the water is still, oxygen is hard to find. A clownfish fixes this problem. It stirs up the water by swimming around in the tentacles. The moving water takes oxygen to the sea anemone. It can breathe again.

Clownfish and sea anemones help each other eat. They help each other survive. They work together. They are one of nature's most incredible animal teams.

GLOSSARY

allies (AL-eyez) creatures that help each other

carnivores (KAHR-nuh-vorz) creatures that eat only meat

coral reef (KOR-uhl REEF) a wall of rock in the ocean

disguise (dis-GIZE) a way of hiding your identity

ecosystem (EE-koh-sis-tuhm) a community of living things

immune (ih-MYOON) not affected by something

mucus (MYOO-kus) a slimy substance made by the body

oxygen (AHK-sih-juhn) a gas many animals breathe to live

poison (POI-zuhn) a substance that can hurt or kill

predators (PRED-uh-turz) animals that hunt other animals for food

species (SPEE-sheez) a certain type of an animal

tentacles (TEN-tuh-kuhlz) bendy arms

waste (WAYST) something unwanted that's released by the body

FIND OUT MORE

BOOKS

Didier, Dominique. *Sea Anemone*. Ann Arbor, MI: Cherry Lake, 2014.

Nagelhout, Ryan. *Clownfish*. New York: Gareth Stevens, 2013.

Neuman, Susan B. *Swim Fish! Explore the Coral Reef*. Washington, DC: National Geographic, 2014.

Rustad, Martha E. H. *Clown Fish and Sea Anemones Work Together*. North Mankato, MN: Capstone, 2011.

WEB SITES

National Aquarium—Anemones
www.aqua.org/explore/animals/anemones

National Geographic—Clownfish and Sea Anemone Partnership
http://video.nationalgeographic.com/video/clownfish_amonganemones

Shedd Aquarium—Thanks, Dad: Anemone Clownfish
www.sheddaquarium.org/blog/2010/June/Thanks-Dad-Anemone
-clownfish

INDEX

B
butterflyfish, 16, 17

C
clownfish, 4, 5, 6–9
   and sea anemones,
     13–21
   what they eat, 17,
     19
   where they live, 5
coral reefs, 5, 7, 8, 11

D
disguise, 5

M
mucus, 14, 15

O
oxygen, 18, 19, 21

P
poison, 13, 15
predators, 7, 9

S
sea anemones, 4, 5, 9
   and clownfish, 13–21
   size, 11

what they eat, 10,
   11, 12
where they live, 5

T
tentacles, 5, 11–15,
   19, 21

W
waste, 19

ABOUT THE AUTHOR

Kevin Cunningham is the author of more than 60 books. He lives near Chicago.

Fabulous Fish

Julie Haydon

Contents

Life in the Ocean	2
The Body of a Fish	3
Schools for Fish	4
Types of Fish	5
Bony Fish	6
Sharks	9
Rays	12
Amazing Shapes	14
Glossary and Index	16

Rigby

Life in the Ocean

Most of Earth
is covered by ocean.

Lots of different fish
live in the ocean.

2

The Body of a Fish

Most fish have scales, fins, and **gills**.

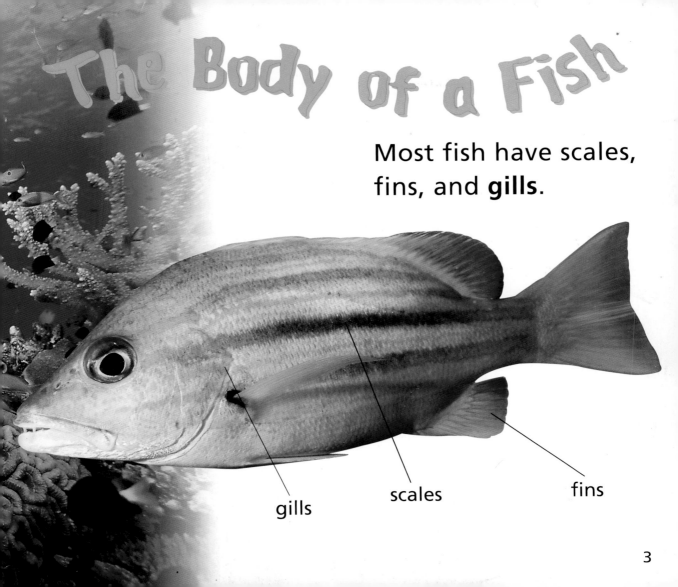

gills

scales

fins

Schools for Fish

Some fish swim in groups
called **schools**.

Types of Fish

There are two main types of fish.

There are fish with skeletons made of bone.
There are fish with skeletons made of **cartilage**.

This fish has a skeleton made of cartilage.

This fish has a skeleton made of bone.

Bony Fish

Bony fish have skeletons
made of bone.

Some bony fish
live in coral reefs.

Eels are bony fish, too.
They hunt at night and hide
during the day in caves and **burrows**.

 **Sharks**

Sharks do not have bones. They have skeletons made of cartilage.

a shark

9

Most sharks are **predators**.
They have rows of sharp teeth.

The great white shark hunts seals, dolphins, fish, and turtles.

The whale shark is the largest fish in the world.

It eats **plankton** and small fish.

a great white shark

a whale shark

Rays

Rays have skeletons
made of cartilage, too.
Rays have flat bodies
with fins like wings.
They flap their fins to move
through the water.

Most rays have their mouths and gills under their bodies.

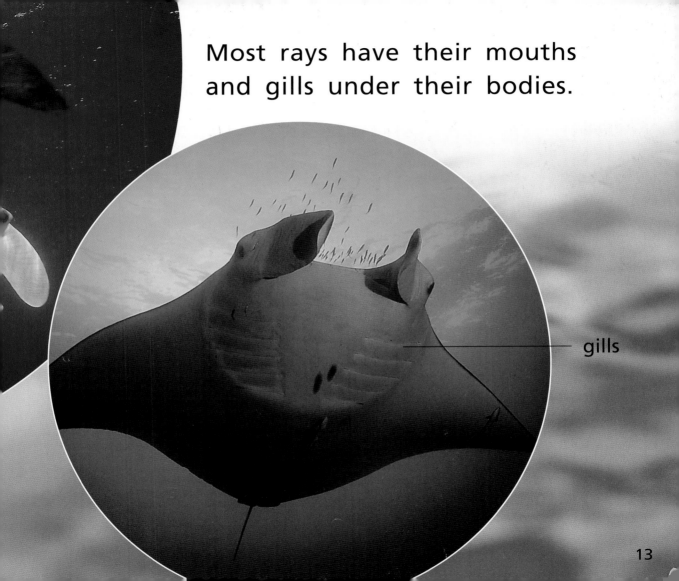

gills

13

Amazing Shapes

Some fish have strange body shapes.

How did these fish get their names?

porcupine fish

swordfish

hammerhead
shark

seahorse

Glossary

burrows holes that animals make to live in

cartilage special body tissue that makes up the skeletons of sharks and rays

gills the part of the body that a fish breathes through

plankton tiny plants and animals that live in the ocean

predators animals that catch and eat other animals

schools groups of fish that swim together

Index

bony fish 6–8

cartilage 5, 9, 12

eels 8

gills 3, 13

plankton 11

rays 12–13

sharks 9–11

skeletons 5, 6, 9, 12